The Efficiency Filing System

THE
Efficiency
FILING
SYSTEM

REVISED AND ENLARGED

L. R. Elliott

BROADMAN PRESS
Nashville, Tennessee

Library of Congress catalog card number: 59–10856

Printed in the United States of America

6. AL 59 K.S.P.

To the memory of my father,
the REVEREND JUDSON ANDREW ELLIOTT, M.A.
to whom I chiefly owe my interest
in theological education
and
to MISS JULIA PETTEE, B.A.,
America's first lady in theological cataloging,
to whom I was most indebted
during thirty-five years
as a theological librarian

Preface

THIS IS A NONSECTARIAN WORK based on professional standards. Seven of the larger denominations are included in the list of Subject Headings, with two general entries each—one ecclesiastical, the other theological. The first of the seven in alphabetic order, Baptists, is also furnished with additional subdivided entries to serve as a guide. On a similar pattern ministers of any denomination can extend their own subject headings as desired. See the Explanatory Notes preceding the List of Subject Headings. A considerable number of specific headings common to several denominations are included. The how-to-do instructions are, of course, intrinsically nonsectarian.

The principles expressed in the American professional literature on classifying and cataloging are the basis for these instructions and subject headings. Attention has been given also to the few works available on ministers' libraries. In the world of learning and libraries subject headings are practically public domain. The index to any scholarly work is an informal list of subject headings. Indebtedness to all this literature is gratefully acknowledged.

The one distinctive idea in this work is simplicity and economy for efficiency. A library that can be contained in an average-sized room and used only by one person, a library amateur, does not need the complex methods and equipment used by professional librarians. This streamline idea runs all through the following pages. Out of thirty-nine years in local and national theological library work have come this central concept and the procedures here outlined.

This is the second edition of the brochure published with the same title by Broadman Press in 1951. But this is a complete rewriting.

The reader should distinguish between filing and indexing. An index is a device—here, folders and index sheets—for recording decisions regarding what signal—a subject heading—shall be assigned to a given piece of recorded human thought. Filing is merely the mechanical process of placing the indexed record in a systematically predetermined location [a certain folder in a certain drawer] where it can be found quickly when wanted. This work is a guide to both operations.

Indebtedness and gratitude are expressed to Dean Jesse J. Northcutt and Professors H. C. Brown, Jr., Gordon Clinard, and Franklin M. Segler of the School of Theology, Southwestern Baptist Theological Seminary, for generous encouragement and valuable suggestions, and to One who performs the dual role of Mary and Martha to nourish unstintedly soul and body, sustaining brain and pen through the mass of tedious detail.

Notices of errata and suggestions for improvement will be appreciated.

Contents

Part One

The Indexing System

I. SUBJECT INDEXING

An efficient system of indexing all the material in one's private library, small or large, is needed by every Christian worker.

The indexing here described uses subject headings under which to make instantly available all the material collected on any particular subject. Arranging subject headings in alphabetic order brings any subject quickly to view. New subject headings can be added indefinitely without ever disturbing the alphabetic order.

Subject indexing applies to clippings and other brief, unbound pieces as well as to permanently bound books, pamphlets, magazines standing on shelves, and personal manuscripts.

Under these subject headings the subject content of a private library can be most easily, quickly, and inexpensively indexed.

II. INDEXING UNBOUND MATERIAL

Unbound material varies in form, size, condition, and content. It includes anecdotes, broadsides, bulletins, charts, clippings, excerpts, graphs, illustrations, leaflets, memoranda, poems, songs, tracts—anything that is flat and thin.

As this material comes to one's study it is unorganized, miscellaneous, and perishable.

1. Vertical Filing

The material is brought into order, preserved, and made usable by placing each piece in its own vertical filing folder,

1

marked by a subject heading on the tab of the folder (Fig. 1). The size of these folders is usually 9½ by 11¾ inches to hold

FIGURE 1

standard 8½ by 11 inch sheets of paper. Get folders in heavy brown Kraft stock to stand wear. They can be had with full-length tab, one-half, one-third, or one-fifth tab.

The closed bottom edge of folders is double or triple creased, so that instead of coming to a sharp edge that will force the sides to bulge, the bottom can be spread one-half inch to keep the contents even.

An adjustable wood or metal support back of the last folder keeps a file of folders upright in a drawer.

2. Marking

Any piece placed in a filing folder should be (1) identified as to its subject, (2) authenticated as to its source, and (3) physically prepared for filing (Fig. 2).

(1) *Subject identity.*—Any article, clipping, tract, or other piece usually has one over-all subject, although more than one idea may be included. Decide what is the over-all subject. Then choose the best word or phrase by which to express this subject.

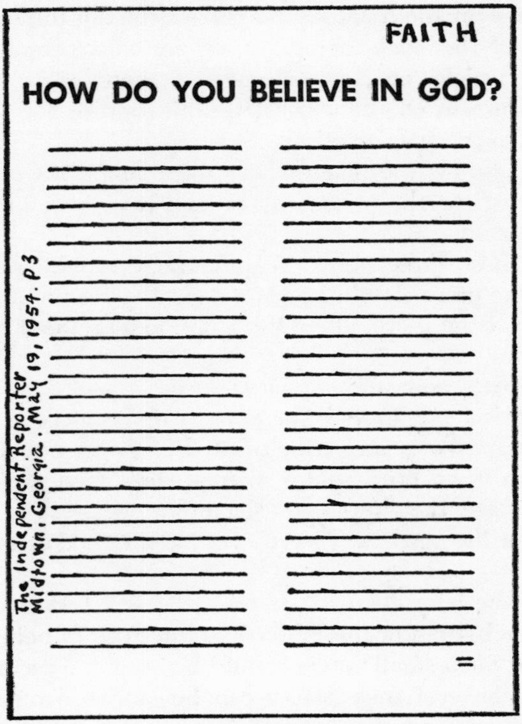

FIGURE 2

The best is that which is brief, most frequently used, and clearly describes the subject. Most of the decision on subject headings has already been made for the user (see the list of Subject Headings beginning on page 42). He will need occasionally to make additional subject headings. Suggestions are given on page 40.

The word or phrase so chosen is printed or typed on the margin of the piece at the upper right-hand corner. Never vary this position. Exactly the same word or phrase, with no variation, is printed or typed on the tab of the folder.

The piece is now identified as to subject (Fig. 2).

(2) *Authentication.*—Any anecdote, illustration, or statement of fact used in public address or writing is more effective if it has the marks of authenticity—who, when, and where.

"Who" means the name of the person making the statement or the name of the book, pamphlet, or periodical from which the statement, article, etc., was clipped or copied.

"When" means the date of the publication or the date of the statement, narrative, or event.

"Where" means the place where the publication originates or the place where the statement or narrative was made or the event occurred.

Any of these three items of authentication which are not already on the piece should be placed on the margin at the upper-left corner of the piece, along the left side margin, or on the bottom margin.

The piece is now authenticated (Fig. 2).

(3) *Physical preparation for filing.*—If the piece is a clipping from a newspaper or magazine printed on paper not stiff enough to stand up in an open folder, then it should be mounted on a stiff sheet. Paste the clipping on the mounting sheet so as to leave a margin for the marks of (1) subject identity and of (2) authentication.

If the piece is quite small, it probably will become crumpled down in the bottom of the folder by larger pieces being dropped down on it. Such small pieces should be mounted on an 8½ by 11 inch sheet. Several such pieces can be mounted on one sheet. The identifying and authenticating marks can be placed on the mounting sheet if the piece does not have sufficient margin itself.

If the piece is folded and stapled to make four, eight, or sixteen pages, open it in the middle and file it so that only half of its thickness adds to the thickness of the contents of the folder. There can be one exception to this rule: If opening the piece in the middle causes its side edges to extend beyond the side edges of the folder, then file the piece closed.

If the piece is a single sheet with margins wide enough for the needed markings and is strong and large enough to stand up of itself, no physical preparation is needed.

All material filed should be reliable, in good literary taste, and relevant to the serious work of the Christian worker. It should mostly supplement rather than duplicate the bound material on the shelves.

3. *Equipment and Process*

Keep in a drawer of the study desk or reading table the tools used in preparing unbound pieces for filing. These tools are scissors, paste, black ball-point pencil, wire stapler, and the improved colorless Scotch tape to mend tears.

Always keep these tools in the same drawer. Use them only for the preparatory process. Thus frustration is avoided and time saved.

Read the piece, whatever form it is. Immediately upon finishing the reading, scan it to determine the over-all subject. Having decided, check the list of subject headings to find the best word or phrase by which to express the subject. Never use a subject heading that is not in the list of subject headings—either printed there or that you have added in the space provided for such additions.

Next, mark the piece, in the manner described above, for subject identity and authentication. Then do whatever physical preparation is needed.

Make a final check to assure that the subject heading on the upper right corner of the piece agrees exactly with that on the tab of the filing folder.

The piece is then ready for filing.

III. INDEXING BOUND MATERIAL

Bound material is books, pamphlets, and magazines in stiff covers that will stand up on a shelf.

Indexing bound material means locating discussions of subjects within the books, pamphlets, and magazines. Classifying the bound volumes for shelf position will be explained later.

The subject contents of bound material should be indexed in the same place (filing folders) with the unbound material. This unified indexing gives the owner the most help for the least cost of time and money.

1. *The Index Sheet*

Use an 8½ by 11 inch sheet of paper of durable quality to withstand frequent handling.

Draw a line (ink) across the sheet one-half inch from the top. From the middle of this line draw a line down to the middle point of the bottom edge of the sheet. This divides the sheet into two equally wide parallel columns. On the back side draw a line from top to bottom down the middle of the sheet. This gives two more equally wide parallel columns. These four columns total more than 40 column inches, 4½ inches wide.

In the middle of the half-inch space at the top of the front side of the sheet print or type the desired subject heading. Its wording must correspond exactly with the wording of the subject heading on the tab of the folder into which this indexing sheet is to be filed.

Some may prefer to run three columns, each 3⅝ inches wide, across the sheet and place the subject heading at the top of the center column. This puts the subject heading directly before the eye when opening the folder.

2. Reading and Indexing

While reading any form of bound material, a person should train his mind to be always alert for useful discussions of any of the various subjects on which he will need help from time to time.

Suppose one is reading a copy of the book on Colossians by Dr. A. T. Robertson, entitled *Paul and the Intellectuals.* Keeping a mental eye open for good discussions on any of the great Christian themes, he comes to page 38 and soon realizes he is reading an illuminating treatment of faith.

Reaching for a sheet already ruled, he enters the subject heading "Faith." Then at the top of the left column he makes the proper entry. All such entries citing a book or pamphlet should include the author's name, the title of the book, the year of publication, if it is a later edition, the year and number of the edition, the publisher, the pages on which the discussion is found, and a note describing briefly the aspect of the subject discussed (Fig. 3).

Below this entry is also shown in Figure 3 the information used to cite an article in a magazine. First is the title of the article, next the name of the writer, followed by the name of the magazine, and, last, the citation of the issue and page numbers.

FAITH	
Robertson, A.T. Paul and the Intellectuals (Colossians) 1928. S.S. Board. p. 38-39. A definitive description of faith and its relation to love.	
Rankin Reunion at Ridgecrest. H.C. Moore Home <u>Life</u> 4(3):8-9, 31 March, 1950. How faith produced strong characters in a notable Baptist family.	
The Faith of a Surgeon. W.D. Lovelock-Jones <u>Baptist</u> <u>Quarterly</u>, London. 14: 291-303. July 1952. Out of a 25 year experience he holds all true healing is of God; only faith can triumph over disease; cites examples.	
Birds and Lilies. John Doe. cf. Matt. 6:25-34 in folder. Matt 1-14; on faith in God for the physical needs of life.	

FIGURE 3

The correct citation of pages depends on which system of page numbering is used in a particular magazine.

Home Life magazine begins numbering each issue with page 1. When citing such magazines, the number of the volume is first, then the issue number in parentheses; after a following colon the page numbers and the month and year are given. The example shown in Figure 3 means volume IV, issue 3, pages 8, 9, and 31, dated March, 1950.

The other system of page numbering goes continuously through all issues of a volume. Page 1 is the first page of the volume's first issue, and the last page of the last issue is 768 in a volume of twelve issues of 64 pages each. For example, 18:249–53, Je '49, means volume 18, pages 249 to 253, in the June, 1949, issue. For a live example, see Figure 3.

Observe that a colon (:) always precedes the page numbers.

A brief note appended to each entry, when consulted later, will help the user to decide if he can use the article without his having to reread it. These entries with added notes should be made as soon as the passage or article has been read. While the impression is fresh in the mind, one can make a better entry more quickly than at the illusive "more convenient season" when the impression has faded. *Always do it now.*

If the user will make these entries in fairly small hand-printed letters, he should average seven entries in a column. Four columns a sheet gives twenty-eight entries. This means a quick inexpensive index to the bound material, revealing twenty-eight good passages on a single subject. A second sheet marked "FAITH No. 2" will index twenty-eight more citations. A third sheet, "FAITH No. 3," will total eighty-four citations. Three sheets use little perceptible space in a filing folder.

Eighty-four citations will, for most Christian workers, probably be more than the maximum they will need for any one subject heading.

IV. INDEXING THE BIBLE

Books of the Bible and chapters, passages, or verses in them should be regarded as subject headings.

If the user's collection is small, a folder for each book of the

Bible will be enough. All entries on any one book of the Bible as a whole, and on all parts of it, are to be filed in the folder bearing the name of the book.

A question of sequence of the folders arises concerning names of books of the Bible when used as subject headings. Most Christian workers have memorized the order of the books in the usual Genesis to Revelation sequence. They may naturally think of placing the folders in the filing drawers in the same sequence. But experience will prove this to work troublesome complications.

The alphabetic sequence will work better in a file where all the other folders are in alphabetic sequence. The following subject headings, selected at random, will illustrate this unified alphabetic sequence.

Acts, Book of	Idolatry
Beatitudes	Isaiah, Book of
Chronicles, 1–2	Lord's Prayer
Counseling	Matthew, Gospel of
Drama, Religious	Old age
Ephesians, Book of	Philosophy
Evolution	Teaching
Faith	Timothy, 1–2
Graded choirs	War
Habakkuk, Book of	Zechariah, Book of

If a folder on any book of the Bible becomes full, then make a second folder with the chapters divided about equally between them. A third folder can be added later with appropriate change of the chapter separations on the folder tabs.

The indexing sheets in the nonbiblical subject folders can refer to material filed in the Bible text folders. For example, suppose one has clipped an illuminating discussion on faith as expressed and implied in Matthew 6:25–34. If the form of the discussion is a commentary on the passage in Matthew, it will be filed in the folder labeled "Matthew 1–14" (Fig. 4). But if it also has helpful suggestions on faith as a subject, then make an entry thus: "*Birds and Lilies* by John Doe, on Matthew 6:25–34, in folder 1–14" (Fig. 3).

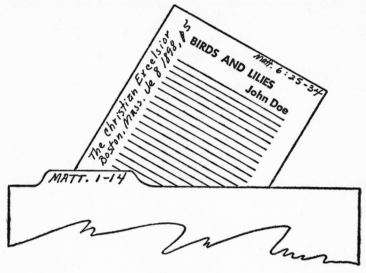

FIGURE 4

The reverse course of action should also be taken when needed. Suppose a sermon in a book of sermons or in the owner's own manuscript file (sec. VII) should contain a helpful reference to Matthew 17:19–20. Enter on the "Matthew" index sheet a reference to the sermon, giving its title, author (if not the owner), and the subject heading under which the sermon is filed or the book in which it is published (Fig. 5).

V. INDEXING BIOGRAPHY

The procedure for indexing biographical material is essentially the same as for indexing unbound pieces and bound volumes.

There is one important difference when indexing individual biographical material, unbound or bound: the alphabetic sequence is based on the name of the subject, not on the name of the author.

1. Individual Biography

Clippings and other unbound pieces about one person will go into a filing folder with the name of that person on the tab of the

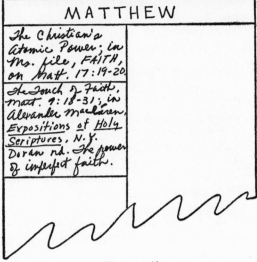

MATTHEW

The Christian's
atomic Power; in
Ms. file, FAITH,
on Matt. 17:19-20.
The Touch of Faith,
Matt. 9:18-31; in
Alexander MacLaren,
Expositions of Holy
Scriptures, N. Y.
Doran nd. The power
of imperfect faith.

FIGURE 5

folder. The name becomes a subject heading. A paragraph or a
chapter about this person in a bound volume is to be entered on
an indexing sheet headed with the name of the person and
placed in the folder labeled with the same name (Fig. 6).

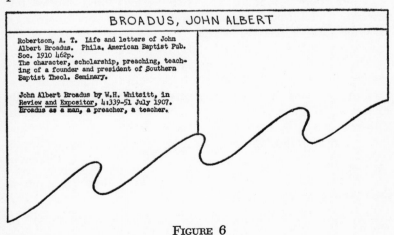

BROADUS, JOHN ALBERT

Robertson, A. T. Life and letters of John
Albert Broadus. Phila. American Baptist Pub.
Soc. 1910 462p.
The character, scholarship, preaching, teach-
ing of a founder and president of Southern
Baptist Theol. Seminary.

John Albert Broadus by W.H. Whitsitt, in
Review and Expositor, 4:339-51 July 1907.
Broadus as a man, a preacher, a teacher.

FIGURE 6

The same indexing sheet also will cite any bound volume about this person (Fig. 6).

2. *Collected Biography*   (*Fig. 7*)

When indexing information about two or more people discussed in the same article in a clipping or other unbound piece, follow these steps:

(1) After marking the piece (using only the name of the person mentioned or discussed first), place it in a new folder labeled only with the name (surname first) of the person discussed first; his name thus becomes the subject heading on both the piece and the tab of the folder in which it is filed.

(2) On the tab of another folder print the name (surname first) of the second person mentioned or discussed in the piece.

(3) On the top of a new indexing sheet print the name (surname first) of this second person (his name thus becoming another subject heading).

(4) Word the entry concerning the second person on the index sheet so as to refer to the piece in the folder labeled with the name of the first person.

(5) Place the second person's index sheet in the folder bearing the same name on its tab.

(6) If there are more than two persons discussed in the same piece, treat each name, separately, in the same manner as described for the second person.

(7) Additional information about any of these names can later be placed in the folders already prepared, unbound pieces being marked and placed in the proper folder and information discovered in the bound volumes being cited on the index sheet already in use in its folder.

VI. INDEXING PICTURES, POEMS, SONGS

Index these various kinds of pieces in the same manner (described in sec. II) as for any kind of unbound piece going into a filing folder.

Pieces of any of these three kinds should not go into folders labeled "Pictures," "Poems," or "Songs." Folders labeled with any

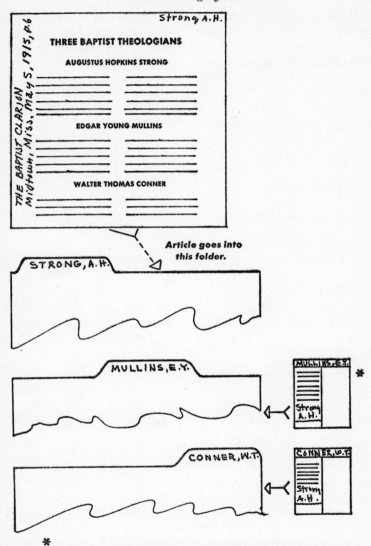

These index sheets refer to the article in the folder marked "Strong, A. H."

FIGURE 7

of these three terms as a subject heading are to be used only for general information about these subjects. This information may include sources of such material; biblical, historical, literary, or other qualities possessed or described; how to use this kind of material effectively; and other such general information or criticism.

Each piece itself is to be filed in the folder with the subject heading that describes the main thought of the piece, whichever of the three kinds it happens to be. For example, the folder labeled "Faith" will contain not only clippings, leaflets, and the like; but it also will have pictures, poems, or songs on faith, and on the index sheet or sheets citations to passages about faith in one's bound material (sec. III), to notable Bible passages on faith (sec. IV), to biographical material on great men of faith (sec. V), and to one's own manuscripts on faith (sec. VII).

The total accumulation is a varied collection of material on a vital Christian theme conveniently assembled and quickly available.

These instructions assume that pieces of the three kinds will be filed in the usual vertical file folders. This kind of filing will be best for pastors and all other Christian workers whose activities do not require them to gather a large collection of any of these three kinds.

Some workers in elementary and secondary religious education may wish to have a large picture file. They may need special equipment. The Baptist Sunday School Board in Nashville, Tennessee, or the nearest Baptist Book Store can suggest suitable equipment and filing practice.

Those church musicians who have, or purpose to acquire, a large collection of published octavo music may wish a more expanded indexing system for their special collection. Such is provided by the Church Music Department of the Baptist Sunday School Board. It is described and illustrated in their pamphlet *The Church Music Record System,* pages 14–16. Their Music Library Cards are standard 3 by 5 inches. They are printed so that a piece of music or a disk record can be indexed under three heads—title, character (subject), and composer. Music indexed thus can be located quickly.

VII. INDEXING MANUSCRIPTS

For the sake of brevity and convenience four forms of personal composition—addresses, lectures, sermons, and talks—whether written in full or only as notes or outlines, will be referred to in this chapter as manuscript or manuscripts, using the abbreviations MS and MSS.

Indexing one's own MSS by alphabetic subject headings is better than numerical (serial or chronological) indexing.

Numbers are meaningless in themselves. In order to find a MS on any subject, one must index the numbered file by some kind of additional indexing in order to find the number under which the desired MS is filed. This is unnecessary—a waste of effort, time, and money. MSS indexed by subject headings filed in alphabetic order need no additional indexing in order for a person to locate a MS on any particular subject.

Each MS should be indexed with a subject heading that expresses the main thought of the MS. The title of the MS, with rare exceptions, should not be indexed. Titles are likely to be occasional, metaphorical, or fanciful. Such expressions do not have the relevance or permanence to make good subject headings for indexing. Also, titles would have to be indexed under their first word and such words too often do not suggest the main thought of the MS.

The subjects of Christian revelation and experience do not change—"now abideth faith, hope, love." The various forms of Christian work and worship acquire permanent expressions by which they are commonly known. Successful indexing must be based on enduring and well-known expressions. Out of these are useful subject headings made (Fig. 8).

Personal MSS may be filed by vertical filing (in drawers) or in loose-leaf books.

1. Vertical Filing

Vertical filing may use one of three kinds of containers—folders, envelopes, or wrappers.

(1) *Folders.*—Vertical filing of MSS in folders under the same subject headings with other unbound material would be the sim-

FAITH
Subject heading

Title   *The Atomic Power of the Christian*

Text   *Matthew 17: 19-20.*

Scripture reading

| Expos. | Text ✓ | Topic | Biog. | Devo. | Didac. | Evang. | Miss. |

Deliveries

| Place | Date | Hour | Results |

Sources and Materials Used

FIGURE 8

plest method. But this may not appeal to some because their own
writings stand out more sharply in their minds than all the other
contents of their libraries. Those who prefer to retain the convenience of filing in folders but wish to distinguish their MS file
from their general folder file may do so easily.

Buy the usual letter-size folders with the tab running the full length of the folder top (full cut rather than third cut or fifth cut). Cut this folder half in two from top to bottom. The result is two folders 6 by 9½ inches. These folders will hold the usual size MS paper when it is cut in half (5½ by 8½ inches), standing upright. This position places the subject, title, and text of the MS near the top of the folder where it is most quickly visible.

This arrangement sets up two parallel rows (front to rear of drawer) of filing folders holding 5½ by 8½ inch MSS. The alphabetic sequence (A to Z) will go through the left row, front to rear, and then continue through the right row, front to rear. The front folder in the right row will follow in alphabetic sequence immediately after the last folder in the left row (Fig. 9).

Cut away the right half of the tab on the first folder, the left half on the second folder, and so on. This operation alternates the tabs so that each subject heading is less likely to be covered by the tab in front (Fig. 9).

The first or front sheet of each MS may be prepared to serve as both an indexing and delivery record form (Fig. 8).

The subject heading on the record sheet will be identical with that on the tab of the filing folder. If one later destroys a MS, the subject heading on the folder tab can be covered with a blank gummed strip and the folder used again.

If the preference is to separate the MS file from all others, use one drawer in a four-drawer cabinet exclusively for this purpose. If one's total vertical file material occupies less than one drawer, keep the MS file (A to Z) in front.

Filing MSS in folders has the advantage of keeping two or more revisions of a MS in the same folder. The various revised MSS can have different titles and different texts but, being on the same subject, they remain in the same folder. This arrangement permits the owner to review quickly the progress of his thought and study on the subject.

(2) *Envelopes.*—Vertical filing of MSS in envelopes is physically practicable if a person keeps only the last revision of a MS on a particular subject. If the MS paper is not larger than 5½ by 8½ inches, two parallel rows of envelopes, open end up, can be placed in a letter-size vertical filing drawer.

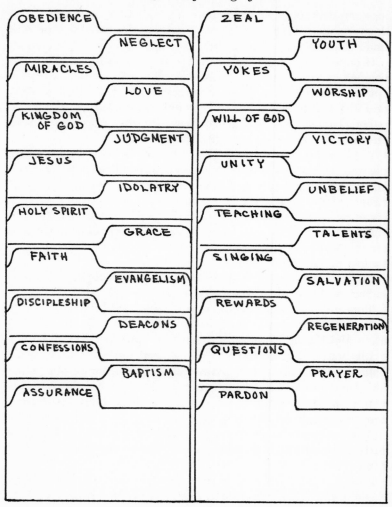

FIGURE 9

Before deciding to adopt envelope filing rather than folder filing, consider these disadvantages of the envelope: envelopes have no tabs to help locate them quickly; an envelope has to be lifted up and out of the drawer; withdrawing a MS from an envelope requires more effort; the envelope has to be replaced in the drawer; quality for quality, envelopes at the present time cost more than folders.

If envelopes are used, cut off the flap. It is not needed on envelopes standing with the open end up.

One may purchase blank envelopes in packages of 100, 500, or 1,000. Get 6 by 9 or 9½ inch envelopes to hold 5½ by 8½ inch paper. The record form one has chosen can be mimeographed on one side of the envelopes.

(3) *Wrappers.*—Vertical filing of MSS in wrappers is a simple and less expensive method than is either the folder or envelope. This wrapper is nothing more than a durable quality of twenty-pound paper, letter size, 8½ by 11. Fold a sheet of such paper so as to make two leaves, 5½ by 8½ inches.

On the outside of one leaf (considered as the front) mimeograph the indexing and delivery record form (as suggested for folders or envelopes).

Fold the wrapper, 5½ by 8½ inches, around the MS, 5½ by 8½ inches, and place it upright in the drawer. As in the case of the folders and the envelopes, there will be two rows of MSS in wrappers in a letter-size filing drawer. The same instruction (p. 17) as to alphabetic sequence also applies to the wrappers.

Like envelopes, wrappers will suffer the disadvantage of not having a tab. This disadvantage can be overcome to a considerable, and probably satisfactory, extent for both envelopes and wrappers by the use of alphabetic guides. Such guides will speed the locating of folders.

These alphabetic guides are permanent equipment. Paying a little more for tough, durable quality will be cheaper in the long run.

2. Subject Indexing in Loose-leaf Books

MSS may be filed in loose-leaf books, also called ring binders. If one accumulates through the years a large collection of MSS, the loose-leaf book form of filing them will be more expensive than vertical filing.

Indexing by subject headings can be done in loose-leaf books as well as in vertical filing in drawers.

Use ruled or unruled hole-punched loose-leaf sheets, 5½ by 8½ inches, in loose-leaf books made for such sheets. Use a good quality of paper, sixteen to twenty pound weight. Cost of loose-leaf books varies considerably, depending on the quality of material in the covers.

Let the first sheet of each MS be unruled paper mimeographed to serve as an indexing and delivery record form. MSS will, of course, be arranged in the loose-leaf book in the alphabetic order of the subject heading in the upper right corner of the cover sheet.

Since these cover sheets will not have a tab, using loose-leaf alphabetic guides will speed the locating of any particular MS. These guides, with punched holes, have tabs extending from the outside long edge of the guides. They are lettered as are the tabs at the top of vertical file guides (Fig. 10).

A one-inch-sized ring binder will hold comfortably a set of A to Z guides and two hundred sheets of paper. A 1½ inch ring book

FIGURE 10

will hold a set of guides and three hundred sheets of paper. Larger ring sizes may be less practicable.

When one book becomes reasonably full, get another book. Keep the first half of the alphabet, guides and MSS (probably from *A* to *L*), in one book, and place the remaining guides and MSS in the second book. When a third book is needed, divide guides and MSS about one third each among the three books. A one-fourth division will be made when a fourth book is needed. This fractioning process can continue indefinitely.

If more than three or four books are used, get guides with multiple alphabetic subdivisions—as *Aa-Ag, Ah-Ap, Aq-At, Au-Az*, etc.

Several books may easily be kept in alphabetic order by placing the books on the shelf, fore edge out, so the guide tabs can be seen.

VIII. SUMMARY ON INDEXING

Now grasp the total picture—a simple but inclusive indexing system using subject headings as the organizing, central element.

The owner has one or more filing drawers of standard letter size. From the front to a point back in the drawer is a row of filing folders standing upright. Each tab bears a distinctive subject heading which stands in alphabetic sequence between the folder in front and the one behind it.

In these folders is a variety (in form) of pieces, each bearing on its upper right corner the same subject heading that is on the tab of the folder. In the folder is all the unbound material on that one subject which has come to the owner's attention.

But this is not all.

On the indexing sheet, or sheets, bearing the same subject heading and filed in the same folder, is a record of all the owner has read on the subject in any of his bound volumes (sec. III).

Also, all he has prepared and delivered on the same subject is indicated on the MS indexing sheet (sec. VII).

Furthermore, as discussions in bound volumes or in unbound pieces on new subjects come to his attention, he can turn to the list of Subject Headings (p. 42); find the appropriate wording for the new subject heading; mark it on the tab of a new folder;

file the first piece (properly marked, pp. 2–4) or the first entry on a new indexing sheet (marked with the same subject heading, p. 6) in the new folder; drop the folder into its alphabetic position in the drawer; a new subject is ready to grow and serve.

The index sheet in any folder can refer to any piece in any other folder as well as to bound material or loose-leaf books on the shelves.

The whole system is indefinitely expandable as to subject headings. The alphabetic sequence of the folders is always in order.

Thus the owner has simply and inexpensively brought together in one place, available at any time and quickly accessible, indexed guidance to all the material he has ever seen in his library or that he has produced on any subject.

IX. PASTORAL WORK FILE

Some persons, especially pastors, may wish a separate file for personal and church work. The following list of titles, used the same as subject headings, is suggested. Each one will adapt this list to fit his own needs.

Baptisms
Brotherhood
   Boy Scouts, Royal Ambas-
   sadors
Budget and Finance
Building—Equipment
Calendar of Activities
Church Council
Community Service
Counseling—Visitation
Deacons—Other Officers
Denominational Service
Evangelistic Meetings
Funerals
Library
Music
Personal Soul-winning
Recreation—Social
Sunday school
Training Union
Weddings
Woman's Missionary Union
   Girls' Auxiliary, Young
   Woman's Auxiliary

Use filing folders with titles on the tabs. Avoid duplication of similar material filed under subject headings. This is a file of activities, contacts, engagements, plans, and programs of work. The other is a file of discussions of subjects and their principles, theories, personalities, history, and criticism.

Part Two

The Classification of Books

I. THE NEED FOR CLASSIFICATION

It is obvious that the bound volumes (books, larger pamphlets, magazines) must always be kept in some kind of consistent order on the shelves if they are to be quickly located when referred to by an index sheet or when otherwise needed.

There are various classification schemes by which the order of position on the shelves may be made and maintained. The scheme described is practical and efficient for the sole user of a small private library. It is economical in the time and money required to install, maintain, and use it.

II. AN EFFICIENT SCHEME OF CLASSIFICATION

In a small private library all the classification needed is to arrange the books on the shelves in a sequence of subject groups that is logical to the mind of the owner. This means a sequence of groups of books on the shelves, each group being on a single subject and the books within each group arranged in alphabetic sequence of the authors' surnames. Sequence on the shelves means three things: from left to right on each shelf; from top to bottom of each section of seven shelves; from left to right as the sequence moves from section to section (Fig. 11).

No classification marks are needed on the books, because the human mind has a natural gift for remembering a position which is daily in view of the user. When need arises, he will recall readily on which shelf a group of books of a certain subject is located.

This fact also makes unnecessary a card catalog to locate the

FIGURE 11

books. Book marking and card cataloging are expensive and are necessary only for large libraries serving the public, such as college and city public libraries. They are not essential for the sole user of a small library. Few users of this manual will ever have more than two or three thousand volumes.

Let each user decide what to his mind is a logical sequence of classification subjects. Such decision is the key to success in starting and maintaining a classification of groups of books on shelves without book marking and card cataloging.

The following sequence of classification groups is offered as a suggestion toward making one's own list of groups. It is a simplified synthesis of several schemes used in libraries of religious books. It may be used as given here.

III. LIST OF CLASSIFICATION GROUPS

It will be helpful to arrange these groups in a logical sequence under broad divisions and subdivisions, as follows.

General and Reference
    Information
    Linguistics
    Bibliography
    Biography
Christian Thought
    Biblical
    Historical
    Theoretical
Christian Service
    The Church
    Evangelism
    Missions
    Education
    Music
    Social Work
Christian Living
    Languages
    Literature
    Fine Arts

Science
Useful Arts
Recreation
Magazines and Periodicals

The classification groups follow, serially numbered under their respective subdivisions. Let each user select, adapt, and revise to suit his own sense of what is a logical order of groups.

General and Reference
Information
   1. Encyclopedias
   2. Yearbooks
   3. Proverbs, quotations
   4. Atlases
   5. Statistics
Linguistics (English only)
   1. Dictionaries
   2. Synonyms, antonyms
   3. Grammars
   4. Use of words
   5. Writing, style manuals
   6. Reading
Bibliography (Books about books)
   1. General, secular
   2. Religious
   3. Catalogs of publishers
   4. Lists from antiquarian booksellers
   5. Periodical lists and indexes
   6. Library manuals

Biography

Keep all biographies here except those of Bible characters. Let collected biography come first, arranged in the alphabetic order of the author's name. Individual biographies and autobiographies will follow, arranged in the alphabetic order of the name of the biographee. The name of each person in the biography collection will be cited on the appropriate index sheet in its folder in the vertical file. (See discussion in sec. V.)

Christian Thought

Biblical

1. Bible languages (Hebrew-Aramaic, Greek)
   Dictionaries, lexicons
   Grammars
   Concordances
   Texts
   Translations—ancient and modern
   Miscellaneous

2. Whole Bible
   Introductions—canon, text, history, criticism
   Hermeneutics, interpretation
   Study and teaching
   Antiquities, archaeology
   History, geography, chronology
   Biographies
   Commentaries
   Apocalyptic works—biblical and non-biblical
   Miscellaneous

3. Old Testament
   Introductions—canon, text, history, criticism
   Hermeneutics, interpretation
   Study and teaching
   Antiquities, archaeology
   History, geography, chronology
   Biographies
   Commentaries
   Apocrypha and pseudepigrapha
   Miscellaneous

4. Interbiblical Period
   Comprehensive works
   History (before A.D. 70)—Maccabees, etc.
   Religion—Judaism, Jewish theology
   Talmud—Targums, Mishnah
   Jewish rabbinical schools—Halakah, Haggada, Midrashim
   Jewish literature—Philo, Josephus, Apocryphal

Connections and quotations (references to Old Testament in New Testament)

5. New Testament
    (Same subgroups as in Old Testament)

Historical

1. General
    Comprehensive works
    Ancient
    Medieval
    Modern
    Countries—Europe, Asia, Africa, North America, United States, South America, Other (alphabetic order of each country in its area)
    Miscellaneous

2. Ecclesiastical
    Comprehensive works
    Antiquities, archaeology (post-biblical)
    Early church history
    Medieval, crusades
    Reformation, modern
    Church history by countries, including state churches (geographical division as before)
    Councils
    Persecution
    Denominations (alphabetic by name)
    Baptists (divide by national or regional bodies, in alphabetic or geographical sequence as preferred)
    History of Christian literature
    Miscellaneous

Theoretical

1. Philosophy
    Comprehensive works
    Histories of, criticism
    Metaphysics
    Particular philosophies (alphabetic by name)
    Logic, dialectics

Ethics, morality, conscience
Aesthetics
2. Religion
Comprehensive works
Histories of, criticism
Philosophy of religion
Antireligious systems—atheism, agnosticism, skepticism, infidelity, rationalism
Non-Christian religions (alphabetic by name)
Non-Christian religions and Christianity compared
3. Theology, Christian
Comprehensive works
Natural theology
Historical theology—creeds, confessions, catechisms
Biblical theology
Systematic theology
Particular topics in theology (alphabetic by subject)
Polemics (modernism versus fundamentalism, science versus the Bible, etc.)
Irenics
Apologetics, evidences
Miscellaneous

Christian Service

The Church
1. Comprehensive works—character of, mission, etc.
2. Constitution—polity, government, autonomy, religious liberty, church and state
3. Ordinances—baptism, Lord's Supper
4. Sunday and weekday services—worship, prayer, Scripture reading, testimonies
5. Administration—officers, business meetings, finance, organizations in relation to the church, building, furnishings, maintenance, etc.
6. Relationships—community, denomination, world, publicity
7. Country, town, and city churches—problems, methods, ministries

8. Pastoral ministry—funerals, weddings, visitation, counseling
9. Preaching, homiletics
10. Sermons, sermon aids

Evangelism

1. Comprehensive works
2. Histories, criticism
3. Biblical
4. Methods—personal, public, revivals
5. Literature—tracts
6. Finance
7. Conserving results

Missions

1. Reference works—reports, statistics, atlases, yearbooks, etc.
2. Comprehensive works
3. Histories, criticism—general, by denominations, other groups
4. Biblical teaching
5. Promotion and support—missionary education, literature
6. Administration—boards, finance
7. Fields—city, state, home, foreign, minorities and special groups
8. Methods—evangelistic, literary, educational, medical, agricultural, industrial, audio-visual
9. Missionary literature, stories

Education (General and Religious)

1. Reference works
2. Comprehensive works
3. Histories of, criticism (may be arranged by countries)
4. Principles, theories of
5. Functions
   Worship
   Prayer
   Evangelism

Missions

Counseling—character growth, vocational guidance

6. Administration

 General treatises

 Sunday school

 Training Union

 Vacation Bible school

 Weekday church school

 Other activities

 (Subdivide by age groups—Elementary, Adolescent, Young People, Adult, Extension Department.)

7. Psychology—general, religious, biblical, age groups as under Pedagogy

8. Pedagogy, teaching

 General

 Elementary

 Adolescent

 Young People

 Adults

9. Teaching Methods

 General—lecture, question, etc.

 Storytelling

 Drama, pageants, choral reading

 Visual—slides, movies, pictures

10. Curriculum material

 General

 Sunday school

 Training Union

 Vacation Bible school

 Weekday schools

 (Each of these may be divided by age groups as under Pedagogy.)

 Other denominations—principles, methods, materials

11. Special days and occasions

 New Year's

 Easter

 Mother's Day

 Father's Day

      Patriotic
      Promotion Day
      Thanksgiving
      Christmas
      Other special occasions

12. Institutions
      Home
      Community—Boy Scouts, Girl Scouts, Camp Fire Girls, day nursery, kindergarten, schools
      Church—Sunday school, Training Union, Vacation Bible school, weekday school, Woman's Missionary Union, Baptist Brotherhood, Baptist Student Union, etc.
      Colleges and universities
      Theological seminaries
      Assemblies, encampments
      Libraries

Music

1. Reference works—dictionaries, yearbooks, directories, catalogs, bibliographies
2. Comprehensive works
3. Histories, criticism, appreciation
4. Psychology, philosophy, aesthetics
5. Physics, acoustics
6. Theory—analysis, composition, conducting, counterpoint, dictation, ear training, form, harmony, notation, sight singing
7. Ministry of music—home, school, religion, church, worship, evangelism, missions
8. Hymnology
9. Hymnals and gospel songs (alphabetic by title)
10. Special occasions
      Funerals, weddings
      Sunday school
      Evangelism, missionary
      Special days (see list under Education)
11. Voice and vocal collections
      Study and teaching

Solo
Duets
Trios
Quartets
Choruses, ensembles
12. Instruments and instrumental collections
    Study and teaching
    Band, orchestra
    Individual instruments (alphabetic by name)
    Records and record players, collections of

Social Work

1. Reference—directories, statistics
2. Comprehensive works
3. Histories, criticism
4. Social movements, institutions, and programs—welfare, reconstruction, reformation, utopias, communal settlements, good will centers, Red Cross
5. Christianity and social work—social gospel, Bible teaching, Salvation Army, Volunteers of America, YMCA, YWCA, etc.
6. Social problems
   Home—parents and children, courtship, divorce, birth control
   Community—public health, parks and playgrounds, hospitals, urban renewal, traffic, public utilities, aged, handicapped, dependents, drunkenness, drug addiction
   Racial problems—general works, Indians, Spanish-speaking, Negroes, other minorities, anti-Semitism, Ku Klux Klan, segregation
   Crime and criminals—delinquency, vagrancy, penal institutions
7. Political science—government, democracy, monarchy, anarchy, socialism, fascism, communism, nationalism, international relations, war, peace
8. Jurisprudence—laws, constitutions, courts, parliaments, property, personal rights, slavery, international law

9. Economics—land, property, wealth, capitalism, finance, currency, stocks and bonds, business, industry, corporations, trusts, monopolies, commerce, tariffs, advertising, insurance, labor and labor unions, migrants, taxation

Christian Living

Languages

1. Classical—Greek, Latin, modern Greek
2. Other European languages (alphabetic by name of language)
3. Oriental languages (alphabetic by name)
4. Other languages
   (Under each language place dictionaries, grammars, texts, etc.)

Literature

1. Reference works
2. Comprehensive works
3. Histories, criticism
4. Literary forms—poetry, fiction, drama, essays, short stories, history, biography, etc.

Fine Arts

1. Reference works
2. Comprehensive works
3. Histories, criticism
4. Description, appreciation, aesthetics
5. Art forms—architecture, decorating, design, drama, theater, drawing, engraving, etching, lithography, mosaics, painting, photography, pottery, sculpture

Science

1. Reference works
2. Comprehensive works, theory
3. Histories, criticism
4. Basic Sciences
   Mathematics

        Astronomy
        Physics
        Chemistry
5. Earth Sciences
        Geography, hydrography
        Geology, mineralogy
        Agriculture, horticulture
6. Life Sciences
        Biology, zoology, botany, heredity
        Physiology, health, medicine, hygiene
        Anthropology, ethnology

Useful Arts

1. Reference works
2. Comprehensive works
3. Histories, criticism
4. Arts and crafts
5. How-to-do, tools—hand, power
6. Materials—cloth, fiber, glass, metal, paper, plastic, wood
7. Products—appliances, clothing, finishes (paint, lacquer, shellac, varnish, wax), furniture, play and sports equipment, tools, toys
8. Homemaking, domestic science, cooking
9. Hobbies

Recreation

1. Reference works
2. Comprehensive works
3. Histories, criticism
4. Amusements
5. Athletics, sports
6. Camping, travel
7. Play, playgrounds, games, gymnastics

Magazines and Periodicals

Arrange in alphabetic sequence of the first main word of the magazine title, ignoring the articles *a, an, the.*

For most private libraries one should not attempt any subdivision of magazines based on subject, frequency of publication, or other consideration.

For a few exceptionally large collections of magazines a person might make a broad division between general and religious. Such division should not be made until one has factual reasons that such division will save time in usage.

IV. OTHER CLASSIFICATION SCHEMES

There are many schemes of classification for libraries. They are found all over the world and go back to ancient civilizations.

One scheme used by some large university and other libraries is that in operation at the Library of Congress. It is a very comprehensive plan providing for many widely varied classes of books.

Another is the Union scheme developed in and for the library of Union Theological Seminary, New York City. This library has well over 300,000 volumes. The Union scheme is suitable for large collections in religion.

The scheme probably best known in America was invented by Melvil Dewey, 1874–76, while librarian of Amherst College. It is used by most college and public libraries. Although it has some faults—as have all the others—it is well adapted to any library having all the classes of knowledge and used by the public. It employs figures to represent the various classes of books and to indicate the sequence of the classes. The notations are constructed with three figures to the left of a decimal point and as many figures as are needed to the right of the decimal point. Hence, the Dewey scheme is also known as the "decimal classification."

Although the decimal scheme is well known and even recommended by a few library manuals for Christian workers, it is not recommended in this work for the following reasons.

Few Christian workers have or will have a library large enough to require the decimal scheme. It has many classes not needed for a small, special collection in religion. It is balanced for all the classes of human knowledge. Hence it is unbalanced for the relatively few classes in Dewey which are needed by the Christian worker.

Its notations do not provide numbers for many classes needed by the Christian worker's specialties.* Or if they are added, they will often be long and unwieldy.

To apply and maintain the decimal scheme one would need the *Dewey Decimal Classification and Relative Index,* which is a very large and expensive book. Much time would be expended initially and continually in finding the right number and marking it on the book.

Another objection is that it brings together classes the Christian worker needs separated and separates those he needs near each other.

In a small collection used by one person the decimal scheme will cost more time and money than it is worth to the user.

---

* Another manual which does recommend the Dewey scheme has added fifty-two subjects to the Dewey class "200 Religion."

Part Three

Subject Headings

I. EXPLANATORY NOTES

1. The Printed Subject Headings

These subject headings are recommended for use on the tabs of the filing folders and their corresponding index sheets. Note two points: (1) Use each heading only as needed, i.e., as material is acquired for the first time on a new subject; (2) always place a check mark on the left of the new heading. If the user consults this list often, these marks will tell him on what subjects he has material.

Observe the differences in the forms of subject headings. Some are simple, one-word headings; some are compound headings; others are complex headings. The simple headings, like "Benedictions," need no explanation. The compound headings, like "Art and Religion," "Christ in Poetry," and "Day of Atonement," are also self-explanatory. So are headings modified by an adjective, as "Domestic Relations." Variations in the form of headings that apparently ought to follow the same pattern are due to popular use rather than to any logic of meaning.

The complex headings are of five kinds. Each kind is distinguished by a sign that saves space. The five signs are: (1) the comma, (2) the parentheses, (3) the dash, (4) the single colon, and (5) the double colon. Any of these five signs separate the main heading before the sign from the subordinate terms which follow the sign. The meanings of these five signs are as follows:

The comma indicates an inverted heading, which is a noun followed by an adjective, as "Christianity, Primitive." This form keeps all the main headings together and indicates the particular phase of each.

The parentheses perform a similar function. They usually enclose a noun and limit the main heading to a particular area, as "Adoption (Theology)," i.e., not family or parliamentary adoption.

The dash indicates a subdivided heading where a broad subject, before the dash, is broken down into natural divisions, as "Bible—Antiquities," "Bible—Chronology."

The single colon is the sign for *See*, e.g., "Agape:Lord's Supper" means "Agape. *See* Lord's Supper." The first heading is not recommended for use in filing. If more than one heading follows, e.g., "Affection:Friendship; Love," the user must decide which of the following headings better suits the subject matter to be indexed.

If the user prefers the opposite arrangement, let him so indicate by reversing the *See* sign in each heading where it occurs in the printed list; for example, the heading "Worry:Anxiety" may be changed to read "Anxiety:Worry" by reversing the words.

The double colon is the sign for *See also*, e.g., "Church::Christianity" means "Church. *See also* Christianity." The *See also* sign brings together headings that describe subjects which have some relation to each other but are not equivalent. All headings after the double colon are in their own alphabetic position in the list, to be used when needed.

When a main heading, with one or more *See also* headings, is first put into use, look at the related headings where they occur in their own alphabetic position. Those checked for active use should be checked too where they occur as a *See also* heading to save the user's time in the future.

See also signs can be made of *See* signs by making a double colon of the single one, e.g., "Budgets:Church finance." To do so change the single colon to a double colon and make the reverse entry under "Church finance." This process changes any *See* reference into a *See also* reference.

Finally, two service signs are used. They are the plus sign and the semicolon. The plus sign, used to save space, indicates the shortened form of a longer heading, e.g., "Adversity:Joy+" or

"Atheism::Belief+." Turning to their alphabetic positions, the user will find the full forms to be "Joy and Sorrow," "Belief and Unbelief." The semicolon indicates only grammatical separation of co-ordinate headings, e.g., "Christ::Christianity; Salvation; Trinity." These three co-ordinate headings tell the user that material on Christ might be found under one or more of the three headings separated by the semicolons.

2. Making Additional Subject Headings

If the printed list does not contain a heading needed to index some new material, let the user make the heading needed. Be sure to record it on the right side of the page opposite the alphabetic position in the list. In deciding how to word a heading, use the forms in the list as examples. Note these points:

Additional subject headings must be consistent; e.g., *Truthfulness* and *Veracity* cannot be used interchangeably. The entry must read either "Truthfulness:Veracity" or "Veracity:Truthfulness," with the second word appearing in its own alphabetic position, right side of the page.

Subdivided headings should be made by the following principles: (1) If one is of major interest, make it the main heading, e.g., "Bible—Archaeology." (2) If the user is equally interested in both subjects, make the more comprehensive one the main subject, e.g., "Christ—Crucifixion." (3) Subjects which show how another subject has been received, evaluated, or used are subheads to the other subject, e.g., "Prayer—History." (4) Subjects which treat the linguistic, literary, religious, scientific, social, or other characteristics of another subject are subheads to the other subject, e.g., "Sermons—Composition and delivery."

Help in making additional subject headings may be obtained from three sources: (1) One's own denominational agencies. Religious, educational, musical, and publishing organizations often can give such aid. (2) Any library nearby. Librarians are happy to assist others with library problems. They have the tools for such service. (3) The following reference works will yield much help on suggestions for subject headings. They are also basic tools for all Christian workers.

THOMPSON, FRANK CHARLES. *The New Chain-Reference Bible.*

Indianapolis: B. B. Kirkbride Bible Co., 1934. Most extensive of its kind. See the copious index.

International Standard Bible Encyclopedia. 5 volumes. Chicago: Howard-Severance Co. 1930. Or one of several one-volume Bible dictionaries. The ISBE index is ample and suggestive.

Oxford Dictionary of the Christian Church. New York: Oxford University Press, 1957.

Concordances to the Bible: Strong's to the AV, 1890; Nelson's to the ASV, 1922; Nelson's to the RSV, 1957.

Twentieth Century Encyclopedia of Religious Knowledge. 2 volumes. Grand Rapids: Baker Book House, 1955.

A good English dictionary and a work on synonyms and antonyms.

3. Omitted Subjects

Subject headings have been omitted in the following areas in order to save space. With the aids suggested, most users will have little difficulty making headings for the subjects indicated in the following six areas.

(1) Names of physical objects used by man. The list contains a few broad subject headings in these areas, as "Bible—Antiquities," "Bible—Natural history," "Church property," "Foods and drinks," "Precious stones."

(2) Names of mental concepts and natural divisions, as chronological periods, geographical areas, named theories or systems of economics, philosophy, politics, psychology, religion, society, and the vices and virtues.

(3) All names in sacred or secular history. When there are two names for one person, use the more familiar one, as Abraham, not Abram. Modern names should be entered in reverse, as Moody, Dwight Lyman. The alternate names and titles for God, Jesus Christ, and the Holy Spirit should be listed under the headings "God," "Christ," "Holy Spirit."

(4) The names of the subheads in numerous broad subject fields, as Bible—Criticism. Those interested in these subjects can devise needed subheads.

(5) The general headings "Church music" and "Religious education" will be sufficient for many ministers, but directors in these

fields will need many specific headings. Their own knowledge and the helps indicated will supply these headings.

(6) Names of human activities, conditions, or experiences, in languages and dialects; literature; occupations, professions, or trades; diseases and remedies; races, tribes, etc.; empires, kingdoms, nations, states; kinds of government; movements or organizations of a civic, cultural, fraternal, political, or social character; churches, denominations, sects, and their respective auxiliary groups (a few are in the list); boards, corporations, or societies for benevolent, educational, missionary, or social welfare service; particular educational institutions; assemblies, conclaves, conferences, congresses, conventions, convocations, councils, diets, sessions, synods (see Convocations+); sacred days and seasons (a few are in the list); historic systems of theology; sacred books, including books of the Bible; controversies (those within a denomination enter as a subhead to that body); the non-Christian religions.

II. LIST OF SUBJECT HEADINGS

Administration (denominational, institutional)::Church administration
Adolescence::Boys; Girls; Youth
Adults
Advent of Christ:Second Advent
Advertising:Church publicity
Affliction:Joy+
Age (Young people, Middle age, Old age)
Agnosticism::Atheism; Skepticism
Alcoholism:Liquor problem
Altars, Christian:Communion tables; Sacrifice; Worship
Amusements:Recreation
Anabaptists
Angel of the Lord
Angels
Annihilationism::Future punishment
Anointing
Anthems::Church music
Antichrist::Satan

Anti-Semitism:Race problems

Apocalyptic literature::Apocrypha+; Daniel, Book of; Kingdom of God; Revelation, Book of; Bible—Prophecy

Apocrypha and Apocryphal books

Apologetics::Authority (in religion)

Apostasy

Apostles::Apostolic age

Apostles' Creed:Creeds and confessions

Apostolic age::Church history—Early church

Apostolic fathers:Fathers of the church

Apostolic succession::Bishops; Church succession; Ordination

Archaeology, Biblical:Bible—Archaeology

Art and religion::Christian art+

Articles of faith:Creeds+

Ascension:Christ—Ascension

Assurance (theology)::Eternal life; Union with Christ

Atheism::Belief+

Atonement::Christ—Person and work; Forgiveness of sin; Sacrifice; Salvation

Authority (in religion)::Bible—Evidences

Baptism::Baptism of infants; Baptismal regeneration; Judaic baptism

Baptism of infants

Baptism of the Holy Spirit

Baptismal regeneration

Baptist Brotherhood

Baptist Student Union

Baptist World Alliance

Baptistries

Baptists::Anabaptists; Freewill Baptists; General Baptists; Primitive Baptists; Seventh-day Baptists

Baptists—Alaska (other areas)

Baptists—Articles of Faith:Baptists—Confessions

Baptists—Church discipline

Baptists—Church government and polity::Church government+

Baptists—Confessions

Baptists—Conventions (e.g., American; Southern; others)

Baptists—Doctrine
Baptists—Education
Baptists—German (other national groups)
Baptists—History
Baptists—Hymns
Baptists—Missions
Baptists—Ordinances::Ordinances
Beatitudes::Sermon on the Mount
Belief and unbelief
Believers::Conversion; Faith
Benedictions
Bereavement::Joy+
Bible
Bible—Addresses, essays, lectures
Bible—Aids to study:Bible—Introduction; Bible—Study+
Bible—Analyses and synopses
Bible—Antiquities::Christian antiquities
Bible—Archaeology
Bible—Astronomy
Bible—Authenticity::Bible—Authority
Bible—Authority::Bible—Evidences
Bible—Chronology
Bible—Covenants:Covenants (theology)
Bible—Criticism (textual, historical, literary)
Bible—Eschatology:Eschatology, Biblical
Bible—Ethics
Bible—Evidences::Bible—Authenticity
Bible—Exegesis:Bible—Hermeneutics
Bible—Geography
Bible—Hermeneutics
Bible—History (in the Bible)
Bible—History (about the Bible)
Bible—Infallibility:Bible—Inspiration
Bible—Inspiration::Bible—Evidences
Bible—Interpretation:Bible—Hermeneutics
Bible—Introduction
Bible—Languages (Aramaic, Greek, Hebrew)
Bible—Literary character:Bible as literature

Bible—Manuscripts:Bible—History (about the Bible)
Bible—Miracles
Bible—Music
Bible—Natural history
Bible—Parallels (Old Testament in New Testament)
Bible—Pictures
Bible—Poetry:Bible—Literary character
Bible—Priesthood
Bible—Prophecy
Bible—Questions and answers
Bible—Quotations::Bible—Parallels
Bible—Science and the Bible::Creation
Bible—Social life and customs
Bible—Study and teaching::Bible—Hermeneutics
Bible—Symbolism and typology
Bible—Teaching:Bible—Study+
Bible—Teachings:Bible—Theology
Bible—Theology::Bible—Prophecy; Bible—Symbolism; God,
  etc. (for particular topics)
Bible—Translation and revision
Bible—Versions
Bible—Old Testament::Bible—(various subheads)
Bible—Old Testament—Canon
Bible—Old Testament Law
Bible—Old Testament—Religion::Bible—Theology
Bible—New Testament::Bible—(various subheads)
Bible—New Testament—Canon
Bible—New Testament—Harmonies
Bible—New Testament Parables:Christ—Parables
Bible—New Testament—Psychology (Jesus, Paul, John, etc.)
Bible and sociology:Social teaching of the Bible
Bible and war
Bible as literature::Figures of speech in the Bible
Bible in art
Bible in Christian experience:Christian life
Bible in literature
Bible in the schools: Religious education and the public schools
Bible reading (private, public)

Bible societies
Bible stories
Birth, New:Regeneration+
Birth, Virgin:Christ—Nativity
Birthright
Bishops::Clergy
Blessing and cursing::Benedictions
Blood covenants:Covenants (theology)
Boasting::Humility+
Body:Mind+
Body of Christ:Church
Book of Common Prayer
Books and reading::Culture
Booths, Feast of:Fasts+
Boy choirs:Church music
Boys::Adolescence; Boy Scouts; Juvenile delinquency
Brotherhoods
Budgets:Church finance
Burdens::Christian life
Burial service::Cemeteries
Burnt offerings:Sacrifice

Calling (theology)::Election+
Camp meetings:Revivals
Canaan, Land:Palestine
Canon:Bible—Old Testament—Canon; Bible—New Testament
    —Canon
Captivity
Caste:Social problems
Casting lots
Catacombs::Cemeteries
Catechisms
Cathedrals::Church architecture
Catholicism
Celebrations and dedications::Rites+
Celibacy::Asceticism
Cemeteries
Ceremonies:Rites+

Chalices
Chaplains (ecclesiastical, hospital, industrial, military)
Character::Christian life; Conduct of life
Character tests::Temptation
Charity::Conduct of life; Orphans
Children:Parent and child
Choirs:Church architecture
Choirs (music)::Church music
Christ::Christianity; Salvation; Trinity
Christ—Ascension
Christ—Atonement:Atonement
Christ—Birth:Christ—Nativity
Christ—Crucifixion
Christ—Death and burial
Christ—Divinity::Trinity
Christ—Humanity and incarnation
Christ—Intercession and priesthood
Christ—Kenosis:Christ—Humanity and incarnation
Christ—Life and ministry
Christ—Lordship
Christ—Messiahship
Christ—Miracles
Christ—Names
Christ—Nativity::**Christmas**
Christ—Parables
Christ—Person and work
Christ—Prayers
Christ—Resurrection
Christ—Sacrifice:Atonement
Christ—Second Advent:Second Advent
Christ—Seven last words
Christ—Sinlessness:Christ—Humanity and incarnation
Christ—Sonship:Christ—Divinity
Christ—Teachings::Christ—Parables
Christ—Trial::Christ—Life and ministry
Christ—Virgin birth::Christ—Humanity and incarnation
Christ in art:Christian art+
Christ in poetry::Bible in literature

Christening:Baptism

Christian antiquities::Church architecture

Christian art and symbolism::Bible—Pictures; Cathedrals; Church furniture

Christian education::Church and education; Denominational schools+; Sunday schools

Christian ethics::Conscience; Sin; Social ethics

Christian evidences:Apologetics

Christian fellowship::Church union

Christian life::Asceticism; Character; Christian ethics; Conversion; Faith; Prayer; Sanctification; Spiritual life

Christian literature::Church history; Fathers of the church

Christian year

Christianity::Apostles; Church; Church history; Christ; Missions; Reformation; Denominations+

Christianity—Evidences:Apologetics

Christianity—History:Church history

Christianity and culture

Christianity and economics

Christianity and other religions::Paganism

Christianity and politics

Christianity, Primitive::Church history—Early church

Christmas::Christ—Nativity

Church::Christianity

Church—Biblical doctrine

Church administration::Administration

Church advertising:Church publicity

Church and education::Christian education

Church and labor::Migrant labor

Church and social problems

Church and state::Religious liberty

Church architecture::Christian art+

Church attendance:Worship

Church calendar

Church committees:Church administration

Church councils:Convocations+

Church covenants

Church decoration and ornament::Christian art

Church dedications

Church discipline

Church entertainments::Christian recreation

Church finance::Stewardship+; Tithing

Church furniture::Altars; Church Decoration+

Church government and polity::Church law

Church guilds

Church history::Church and state; Convocations+; Creeds+; Denominations+; Fathers of the church; Martyrs; Missions; Monasticism and religious orders; Papacy; Persecution; Reformation; Revivals. (Also use as a subhead to the names of countries, e.g., U. S.—Church history.)

Church history—Early church (to about A.D. 600)::Christianity, Primitive

Church history—Middle Ages (to about A.D. 1500)

Church history—Modern

Church history—Reformation:Reformation

Church law

Church libraries

Church membership

Church music::Hymns; Organs+

Church officers:Church government+; Church wardens; Deacons; Elders; Stewards; Vestrymen

Church plate

Church polity:Church government+

Church property::Church furniture

Church publicity

Church schools::Parochial schools; Sunday schools; Vacation church schools; Weekday religious instruction

Church services:Liturgies; Orders of worship

Church statistics

Church succession::Apostolic succession

Church surveys

Church unity:Christian fellowship

Church union::Community churches

Church wardens

Church work::Evangelistic work; Missions; Social service; Sunday schools

Church work, Rural:Rural churches
Churches, Nondenominational:Community churches
Churches—Public relations::Church publicity
Cities and towns::Church and social problems
City churches
City missions
Civil rights::Free speech; Liberty of the press; Religious liberty
Civilization::Anthropology; Culture; Education; Manners+; Religions; Social problems; War+(also as a geographical subhead, e.g., U. S.—Civilization; but as the main heading for a race, e.g., Civilization, Canaanite)
Class discrimination:Social problems
Clergy::Ministers; Parishes+
Close and open communion
Collections (church)
Comfort::Joy+; Sympathy
Communion:Lord's Supper
Communion, Open:Close and open communion
Communion sermons:Lord's Supper—Sermons
Communion tables::Altars, Christian
Communion with God:Spiritual life
Communism::Government
Community churches::Christian fellowship
Comparative religion:Christianity and other religions; Religions
Conduct of life::Christian life; Duty; Ethics; Love; Spiritual life
Confession::Forgiveness of sin
Confessions of faith:Creeds+
Confirmation::Church membership
Congregation::Church
Congregationalists
Conscience::Liberty of conscience; Christian ethics
Conscientious objectors::Pacifism
Consecration of bishops:Ordination
Constitutions (for churches and church-related agencies)
Consubstantiation:Lord's Supper
Controversies:Creeds+; Heresy; Polemics
Conversion::Regeneration
Converts (religious)

Convocations, councils, diets, and synods::individual names in inverted order, e.g., Constance, Council of

Co-operation::Christian fellowship; Church work

Councils:Convocations+

Counseling::Psychology, Pastoral; Vocational guidance

Courage::Fear

Courts, Church:Church discipline

Courtship::Love; Marriage

Covenants::Church history

Covenants (theology)

Covenants, Church:Church covenants

Covetousness

Creation::Evolution; God; Universe

Creeds and confessions::Catechisms (also names of particular creeds and confessions)

Criticism, Theological:Modernism

Cross (theology):Atonement

Crucifixion of Jesus:Christ—Crucifixion

Crusades

Cults (i.e., non-Christian or pseudo Christian religious movements)

Daily Vacation Bible schools:Vacation church schools

Day of Atonement::Atonement

Deaconesses

Deacons

Death

Dedication::Church dedications

Deism::God; Rationalism

Deluge::Bible—Science+

Democracy and religion::Religious liberty

Demonology::Devil

Denominational schools and colleges::Church and education; Parochial schools

Denominations and sects::Cults

Depravity::Fall of man; Sin

Desire

Devil::Demonology

Devotional literature
Dictators::Government
Diets:Convocations+
Difficulties in the Bible:Bible—Questions+
Dioceses
Directors of church music
Directors of religious education
Disciples of Christ
Discrimination::Social problems
Dispensations, Divine::Covenants (theology)
Dissenters:Nonconformists
Divination::Superstition
Divorce::Marriage
Doctrinal theology:Theology
Domestic relations::Divorce; Family
Drama, Religious::Bible as literature

Early church:Christianity, Primitive
Earth::Creation; Geology+; Universe
Easter
Eastern churches
Ecclesiology:Church; Church decoration+
Economics::Capitalism; Communism; Labor+; Land; Popula-
    tion; Property; Socialism+; Wealth
Ecumenical bodies (twentieth century)
Ecumenical councils:Convocations+
Edicts::names of particular edicts
Education::Libraries; Public schools; Religious education; Study,
    Methods of
Elders
Election (theology)::Predestination
Emblems
Emotions
Entertainments:Church entertainments
Episcopacy::Apostolic succession
Eschatology, Biblical::Future life; Resurrection; Second Advent
Eternal life::Immortality; Union with Christ
Eternity::Immortality

Ethics::Character; Christian ethics
Eucharist:Lord's Supper
Evangelical Revival—Eighteenth Century
Evangelistic work::Conversion; Evangelists; Revivals
Evangelists
Evidences of Christianity:Apologetics
Evil::Satan; Sin; Suffering
Evolution::Religion and science
Excommunication
Exhortation::Preaching

Faith::Belief+; Justification; Salvation
Faith cure::Mental healing
Fall of man::Depravity
Family::Domestic relations; Home; Parent and child; Worship,
    Family
Fasting::Fasts+
Fasts and feasts::Christian year
Fathers of the church
Fear::Courage; Reverence
Feasts:Fasts+
Festivals::Christian year; Holidays
Figures of speech in the Bible::Bible as literature; Parables
Flesh, soul and spirit (biblical use)
Flood, The:Deluge
Foods and drinks
Foreigners (Bible):Strangers
Foreigners, Church work with:Missions, City
Foreknowledge of God:Predestination
Forgiveness of sin
Free speech
Free will and determinism
Freewill Baptists
Freedom of religion:Religious liberty
Freedom of speech:Free speech
Freedom of the press
Freedom of the will:Free will+
Freedom of worship:Religious liberty

Friendship::Love; Sympathy
Fundamentalism::Modernism
Funeral service
Future life::Immortality
Future punishment::Hell
Future state:Eschatology

Genealogy
General Baptists
Geography (biblical)
Geology and the Bible::Creation; Earth; Evolution
Gift of tongues::Pentecost
Gifts, Spiritual
Girls::Children: Young women; Youth
Gnosticism::Paganism
God::Atheism; Deism; Holy Spirit; Natural theology; Pantheism;
    Providence+; Religion; Theism; Trinity
God—Attributes
God—Names
God—Sovereignty
Gods::Mythology; Religions
Golden Rule::Conduct of life
Good and evil::Sin
Gospel::Law and the gospel
Government::Church government+
Grace (theology)
Guilt::Sin

Habit::Instincts
Happiness::Joy+
Heathenism:Paganism
Heaven::Future life
Hell::Future punishment
Heredity::Instincts
Heresy::Schism
Heroes::Courage; Martyrs
Higher criticism of the Bible:Bible—Criticism

History::Bible—History (in the Bible); Church history; Civilization; Man

Holidays::Fasts+; also names of holidays

Holiness (Christian):Sanctification

Holy Communion:Lord's Supper

Holy days:Christian year

Holy orders:Ordination; Priesthood+

Holy places:Shrines

Holy Spirit::Pentecost; Salvation; Sanctification; Trinity

Holy Week::Easter

Home::Family

Human relations:Conduct of life

Humiliation of Christ:Christ—Kenosis

Humility and pride

Hymnody

Hymns::Church music

Iconoclasm

Idolatry

Illiteracy::Education

Immersion:Baptism; Baptistries

Immortality::Eschatology; Future life

Imputation (theology)::Justification

Incarnation:Christ—Humanity+

Infant baptism:Baptism of infants

Inquisition::Heresy; Martyrs; Persecution

Inscriptions

Inspiration of the Bible:Bible—Inspiration; Revelation

Installation::Ordination

Instincts

Interbiblical history

Intercession:Prayer

Interchurch co-operation::Community churches; Ecumenical bodies (twentieth century)

Intermediate state::Eschatology; Purgatory

International Sunday school lessons::Bible—Study+

Interpretation of the Bible:Bible—Hermeneutics

Itinerant preaching

Jewish exegesis
Johannine problem:Bible—Criticism
Johannine theology:Bible—Theology
Joy and sorrow::Bereavement; Happiness; Suffering; Sympathy
Judaic baptism::Baptism
Judaism
Judgment
Judgment day::Eschatology; Second Advent
Junior church
Justification::Atonement; Imputation
Juvenile delinquency

Kingdom of God::God—Sovereignty; Christ—Messiahship

Labor and laboring classes::Capitalism; Church and labor; So-
      cialism+
Laity::Congregation; Preaching, Lay
Land::Wealth
Language and languages::Culture
Law::Justice, Social
Law, Mosaic:Mosaic law
Law and the gospel
Lay preaching:Preaching, Lay
Laying of cornerstones
Laying on of hands::Confirmation; Ordination
Laymen:Laity; Men in Christian work
Leadership::Counseling
Learning and scholarship::Culture; Education
Lectionaries::Christian year
Legends::Stories+
Leisure::Recreation
Lent::Easter; Holy Week
Liberty::Civil rights; Religious liberty
Liberty of conscience::Nonconformists; Persecution; Religious
      liberty
Liberty of the press::Prohibited books
Libraries::Books+
Licensure:Ministers—Licensure+

Life::Man
Light and darkness
Liquor problem::Prohibition
Litanies::Book of Common Prayer—Litany
Literature::Culture
Liturgical music:Book of Common Prayer—Music; Chant;
   Church music
Liturgies
Logia::Christ—Teachings
Lord's Prayer::Prayer
Lord's Supper
Lord's Supper—Hymns
Lord's Supper—Sermons
Love (Christian)
Lutheran churches

Man::Anthropology; Creation; Fall of man; Heredity
Manners and customs::Bible—Antiquities; Christian antiquities;
   Rites+
Marriage::Courtship; Divorce; Family
Martyrs::Persecution
Masters and servants::Domestic relations
Medicine and religion::Faith cure
Meditations::Devotional literature
Memorial services
Men in Christian work::Brotherhoods
Mental healing::Faith cure; Medicine and religion
Mental hygiene
Messianic hope:Christ—Messiahship; Kingdom of God
Methodists
Middle age
Middle Ages::Church history—Middle Ages
Middle East
Migrant labor
Militarism::Pacifism
Millennium::Second Advent
Mind
Mind and body::Mental healing

Ministers::Clergy; Evangelists; Pastors; Preachers
Ministers—Call and training
Ministers—Culture, morals, manners
Ministers—Licensure and ordination::Ordination
Ministers—Personal piety
Ministers—Salaries, pensions, etc.::Church finance
Ministers of church music:Directors of church music
Ministers of religious education:Directors of religious education
Minorities::Race problems
Miracles::Faith cure; Supernatural+
Missionaries—Call and training
Missionary methods
Missions (use geographical subdivisions, e.g., Missions—Africa)::
    Evangelistic work; Missionaries+
Missions, Agricultural
Missions—Apologetics
Missions, Associational
Missions, Bible teaching of
Missions, City
Missions, Educational
Missions, Foreign
Missions, History of
Missions, Home
Missions, Industrial
Missions, Medical
Missions, State
Modernism::Fundamentalism
Monasticism and religious orders
Money::Wealth
Monotheism::God; Polytheism
Monuments::Cemeteries
Moral conditions::Social problems
Moral education:Religious and Moral+
Moral law:Christian ethics; Mosaic law; Sin
Moral theology (Catholic)::Christian ethics
Mosaic law
Motion pictures
Music::Bible—Music; Church music

Mysteries, Religious::Paganism
Mysticism::Pietism; Spiritual life
Mythology::Paganism

Names (biblical, Christian)
Natural theology::Apologetics; Deism
Nature worship::Paganism
Necessity (philosophy)::Fate+; Freedom of the will; Predestination
Negroes—Churches and missions
Negroes—Education
Negroes—Music
Negroes—Religion
Neo-orthodoxy::Theology
New birth:Regeneration
New Testament:Bible—New Testament
New Testament church::Church, Early
New Testament Greek:Bible—Languages
New Testament history:Apostolic age
New Testament theology:Bible—Theology
Newspapers::Religious newspapers+
Nonconformists::Brownists; Puritans
Nonresistance::Conscientious objectors; Pacifism
Numbers, Mystic:Symbolism of numbers
Nuns::Convents+; Sisterhoods

Obituaries::Funeral service
Occult sciences
Offerings:Collections (church); Sacrifice; Tithing
Old age
Omniscience of God::God—Attributes; Predestination
Open-air preaching::Revivals
Optimism and pessimism
Oracles
Orders of worship::Liturgies
Ordinances::Baptism; Lord's Supper
Ordination::Apostolic succession; Bishops; Laying on of hands
Organs and organ music::Chimes

Oriental religions::Religions
Orphans::Charity

Pacifism::Conscientious objectors; Peace+
Paganism::Idolatry
Pain::Suffering
Palestine:Bible—Geography
Pantheism::Polytheism; Theism
Papacy::Catholic Church
Parables::Christ—Teachings
Parent and child::Family
Parishes and parish clergy
Parochial schools::Church schools
Pastoral office and work::Church work+; Ministers—Call+
Pastoral psychology:Psychology, Pastoral
Pastoral theology:Pastoral office+
Pastors::Clergy; Ministers; Parishes+; Pastoral office+
Pastor's library::Theology—Bibliography
Patriarchs (Bible)
Patristics:Fathers of the church
Patriotism::Nationalism
Peace and war::War and religion
Pentecost::Fasts+; Gift of tongues; Holy Spirit
Pericopes:Christian year; Lectionaries
Periodicals::Religious newspapers+
Persecution::Heresy; Inquisition; Religious liberty
Perseverance of the saints::Sanctification
Personality::Character; Soul
Philosophy::God; Truth; Universe
Philosophy, Moral:Ethics
Philosophy of the Christian religion
Philosophy of religion
Piety::Christian life
Plays and pageants
Poetry::Hymns; Religious poetry
Poetry of the Bible:Bible as literature
Polemics::Creeds+
Politics and Christianity:Church and state; Social Christianity

Polity, Ecclesiastical:Church government+
Polygamy::Marriage
Polytheism::Monotheism
Practical theology::Church government+; Church work+;
  Evangelistic work; Pastoral office+; Preaching; Sunday
  schools; Worship
Prayer::Christ—Intercession+; Prayers in the Bible
Prayer—History
Prayer Books::Book of Common Prayer; Liturgies; Orders of
  worship
Prayer Meetings
Prayers, Family
Prayers in the Bible
Preachers::Clergy; Ministers; Preaching
Preaching::Itinerant preaching; Open-air preaching; Preach-
  ers; Preaching, Lay; Sermons
Preaching, Lay
Precious stones
Predestination::Election; Freedom of the will
Presbyterian churches
Preservation (theology):Assurance
Priesthood (biblical)
Priests, Christian::Clergy
Priests, Non-Christian::Paganism
Primitive Baptists
Probation after death::Future punishment; Intermediate state
Problems in the Bible:Bible—Questions+
Profession of faith:Church membership
Prohibition::Liquor problem
Prophecies::Bible—Prophecy
Prophecy, Messianic::Christ—Messiahship; Servant of Jehovah
Prophets::Bible—Prophecy
Protestant Episcopal Church in the U.S.A.
Protestantism::Creeds+
Proverbs, biblical and non-biblical
Providence and government of God::Predestination; Sin
Psalmody::Church music; Psalters
Psalters

Pseudepigrapha:Apocrypha+
Psychiatry and religion::Mental healing
Psychology, Biblical::Belief+; Flesh; Mind
Psychology, Pastoral::Counseling
Psychology of preaching:Preaching
Psychology of religion
Public schools
Public speaking::Sermons—Composition+; Voice culture
Publicity:Church publicity
Punishment::Future punishment
Puritans::Nonconformists

Quotations::Proverbs+
Quotations of Old Testament in New Testament:Bible—Parallels+

Rabbinical literature::Jewish exegesis
Race problems::Social ethics
Races (ethnic)::names of particular races
Radio and television, Christian::Preaching; Drama, Religious
Rationalism::Agnosticism; Atheism; Skepticism
Reason::Mind
Reconciliation (theology)::Atonement
Recreation
Records, Church
Redemption::Salvation
Reformation::Protestantism
Reformers (political, religious, social)
Refugees::Persecution
Regeneration (theology)::Conversion
Religion::Belief+; God; Religions; Revelation; Sacrifice; Supernatural power; Superstition; Worship
Religion and science::Bible—Science+; Creation; Evolution; Natural theology
Religions::Christianity; Gods; Oriental religions; Religion; also names of particular religions
Religions—Biography::Christian biography
Religious denominations:Denominations+

Religious drama:Drama, Religious
Religious education::Bible—Study+; Character; Church and education; Sunday schools
Religious education and the public schools::Public schools
Religious liberty
Religious newspapers and periodicals
Religious poetry::Christ in poetry; Hymns
Renaissance
Repentance::Conversion; Faith
Resurrection::Christ—Resurrection
Revelation::Authority (in religion); Bible—Evidences+; Bible —Inspiration; Faith
Revenge
Reverence::Worship
Revivals::Conversion; Evangelistic work
Rhetoric::Bible as literature
Rites and ceremonies::Fasts+
Rural churches::Town and country+
Rural life
Rural schools

Sabbath::Sunday
Sacraments::Ordinances
Sacred books::Bible; also names of other sacred books
Sacrifice::Atonement; Rites+
Saints
Salvation::Atonement; Christ—Person+; Conversion; Redemption; Regeneration; Sanctification
Sanctification::Union with Christ
Sanhedrin
Satan::Angels, Fallen
Schism::Heresy
Science::Religion and science
Second Advent::Millennium
Secret societies
Sects:Denominations+
Segregation:Race problems
Septuagint::Bible—Versions

Sermon on the Mount::Beatitudes; Lord's Prayer

Sermons::Bible—Hermeneutics; Bible—Study+; Preaching

Sermons—Composition and delivery

Sermons for special occasions

Servant of Jehovah

Sessions:Church administration

Seven last words:Christ—Seven last words

Seventh-day Baptists

Sex and religion

Shrines

Sick—Pastoral visits::Joy+

Sin::Antinomianism; Depravity; Forgiveness of sin; Future punishment; Guilt; Salvation

Singing in worship::Church music; Hymns

Sisterhoods

Skepticism::Agnosticism; Belief+

Slavery

Social Christianity::Church and social problems; Social teaching of the Bible

Social ethics::Social Christianity

Social problems::Church and social problems

Social service::Church and social problems

Social teaching of the Bible

Socialism and Christianity

Son of God:Christ—Divinity

Son of man:Christ—Humanity; Christ—Messiahship

Songs (sacred)::Hymns

Soul::Flesh+; Personality; Spiritual life

Soul-winning:Evangelistic work

Speeches and addresses::Sermons

Spires::Church architecture

Spirit::Soul

Spirits, Evil:Demonology

Spiritual life::Christian life; Union with Christ

Statistics::Church statistics

Stewards::Trustees

Stewardship, Christian::Christian life; Tithing

Stories and storytelling

Strangers
Study, Methods of::Teaching
Suffering::Joy+; Pain
Sunday::Sabbath
Sunday schools::Bible—Study+; Junior church
Superintendents::Church officers
Supernatural power::Inspiration+; Miracles; Revelation
Superstition::Occult sciences
Symbolism::Christian art+; Emblems; Typology
Symbolism of numbers
Sympathy::Comfort
Synagogues
Synods:Convocations+

Tabernacle::Temple at Jerusalem
Teacher training::Bible—Study+; Stories+; Sunday schools
Teaching::Education
Temperance::Prohibition
Temples::Church architecture; Worship
Temptation::Character
Ten Commandments
Thanksgiving
Theism::God
Theological education::Ministers—Call+
Theology::Christianity; Church; Creeds+; God; Holy Spirit;
   Christ; Religion
Theology, Biblical
Theology, Doctrinal
Theology, Historical
Theology, Pastoral::Church work
Tithing::Church finance; Stewardship+
Tolerance and intolerance::Religious liberty
Torture:Inquisition
Town and country churches::Rural churches
Tracts, Religious
Trinity::Theology, Biblical
Trust in God::Faith
Trustees::Stewards

Truth::Word of God
Typology::Bible—Hermeneutics

Union with Christ::Spiritual life
United churches:Community churches
United Nations::International relations
Universe::Astronomy; Creation
Universities and colleges::Denominational schools+
Unpardonable sin

Vacation church schools
Vestrymen
Vicarious sacrifice::Atonement
Virgin birth:Christ—Nativity
Vocational guidance::Counseling
Voice culture::Public speaking
Voluntary church principle::Christ—Lordship; Church government+

War and religion::Peace and war
Wealth::Earth; Land
Weddings::Marriage
Weekday religious instruction::Church schools
Will::Freedom of the will
Wills::Wealth
Wine in the Bible::Temperance
Wit and humor::Speeches+
Women in Christian work
Women in the Bible
Word of God::Revelation
World::Creation; Man
World War::Peace+
Worship::Liturgies; Orders of worship
Worship, Family
Writing::Books+

Young men:Young people+
Young people:Adolescence; Youth

Young people and the church
Young women:Young people+
Youth:Adolescence
Youth movements